# SOLOS FOR THE SANCTUARY
# SPIRITUALS

## 7 PIANO SOLOS FOR THE CHURCH PIANIST

Arranged by Glenda Austin

ISBN 978-1-61780-651-3

WILLIS MUSIC

EXCLUSIVELY DISTRIBUTED BY

## HAL•LEONARD®
### CORPORATION
7777 W. BLUEMOUND RD. P.O. BOX 13819 MILWAUKEE, WI 53213

Visit Hal Leonard Online at
**www.halleonard.com**

# FOREWORD

These arrangements really began years ago when I was the teenage pianist at a small Baptist church. My older sister and I were "volunteered" by our mother to play the little spinet piano and the Thomas organ. I must admit that together we had a lot of fun coming up with different twists and variations to the hymns and spirituals we grew up with.

Years later, I continue to love and be immersed in all kinds of music—and, I am still playing the piano at church, although I am now fortunate enough to enjoy a concert Steinway. Each week I may play a prelude, offertory, postlude, solo or other special music that is needed. By my estimate, I've played thousands of church services—so I've enjoyed arranging for many occasions. With the *Solos for the Sanctuary* series, I am very happy to share with you some of my favorite piano arrangements that I've compiled over the years and have recently tweaked for publication. Many of them have a little twist of the Southern Baptist/Methodist flavor that I hope you and your audience will enjoy.

*Glenda Austin*

P.S. My sister is still on the organ. She's also been "upgraded"— and now plays on a Wicks-Quimby 19-rank pipe organ. We still play the occasional duet!

# CONTENTS

# The Gospel Train

African-American Spiritual
*Arranged by Glenda Austin*

**Driving, but controlled**

*f*

*L.H. softer, in the background*
*(lightly pedal as needed)*

*simile*

*mf*

*f*

# Joshua
## (Fit the Battle of Jericho)

African-American Spiritual
*Arranged by Glenda Austin*

Driving and rhythmic

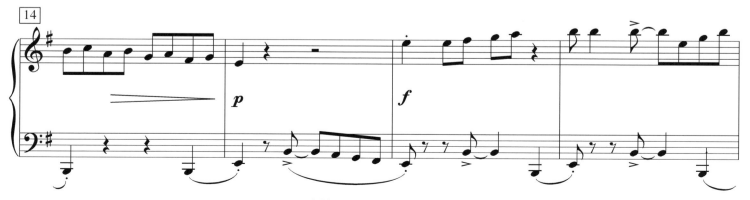

# My Lord, What a Morning

African-American Spiritual
*Arranged by Glenda Austin*

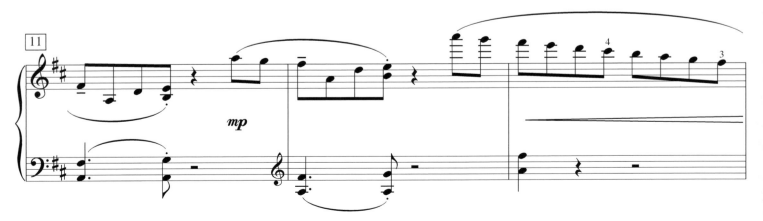

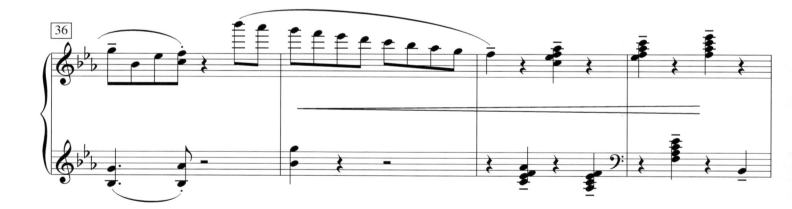

# Rock-A-My Soul

African-American Spiritual
*Arranged by Glenda Austin*

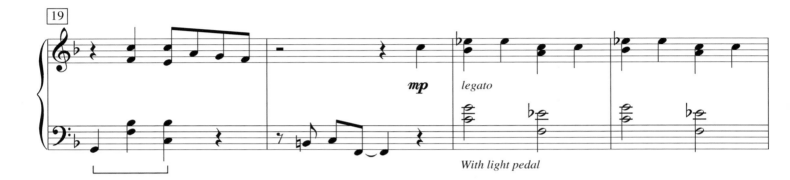

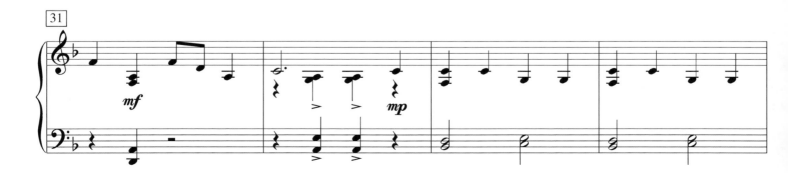

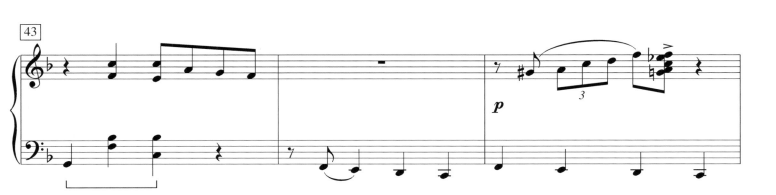

# Swing Low, Sweet Chariot

Traditional Spiritual
*Arranged by Glenda Austin*

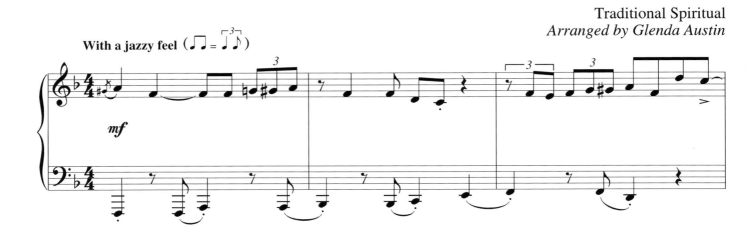

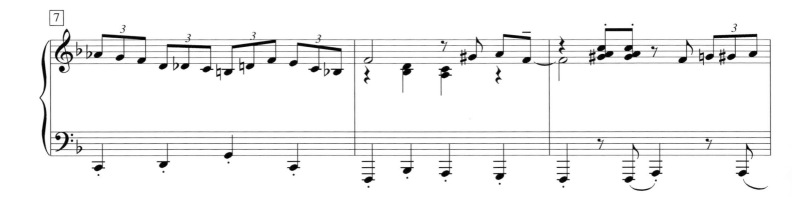

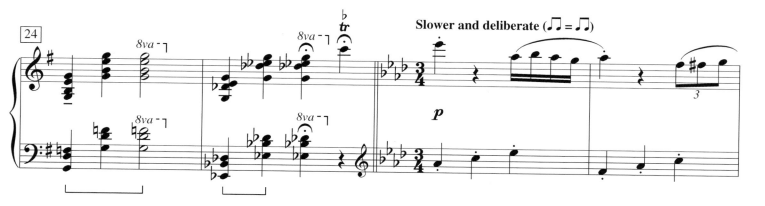

**Broadening, "big band" sound**

# There Is a Balm in Gilead

African-American Spiritual
*Arranged by Glenda Austin*

**Ethereal, with reverence and flexibility**

*With pedal*

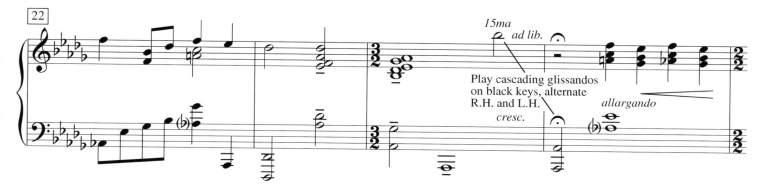

# Wayfaring Stranger

Southern American Folk Hymn
*Arranged by Glenda Austin*

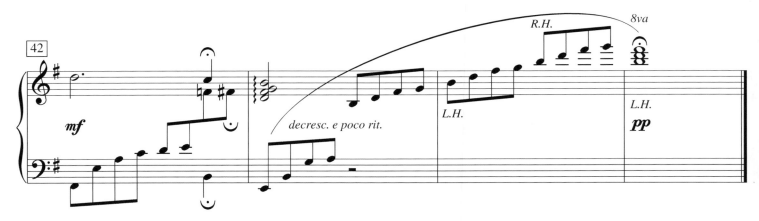